The
Wedding Photographer's
Altar Returns
Check-List

The
Wedding Photographer's
Altar Returns
Check-List

GARY W. CUTRELL

To order additional copies of this book, contact:
Xlibris
1-888-795-4274
www.Xlibris.com
Orders@Xlibris.com
802842

Set-Up

IN: BRIDE

Shot

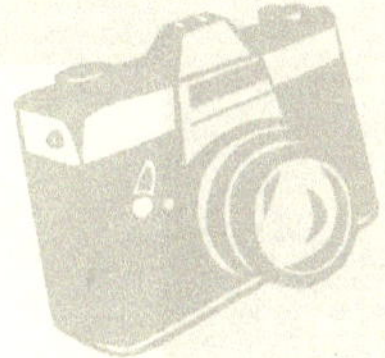

Full Length of Bride

Notes

Set-Up

IN: GROOM

Shot

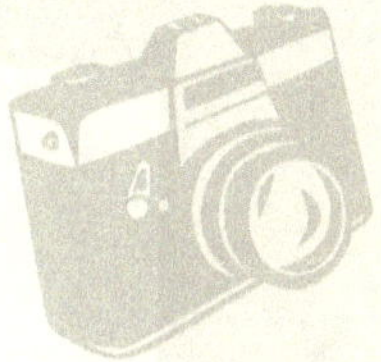

Bride and Groom

Notes

Set-Up

IN: MINISTER

Shot

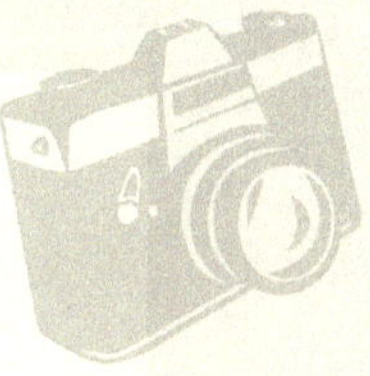

Bride and Groom with Minister

Notes

Set-Up

OUT: Minister
IN: Bride's Parents

Shot

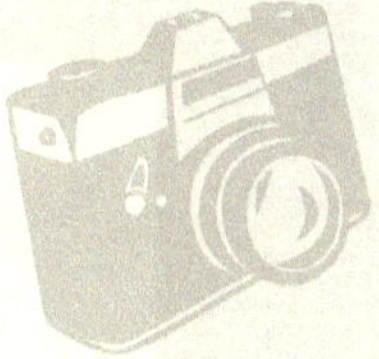

Bride and Groom with her Parents.

Notes

Set-Up

IN: Groom's Parents

Shot

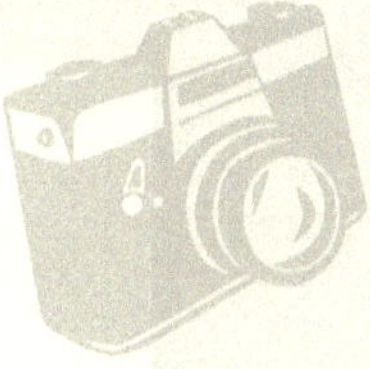

Bride and Groom with All Parents

Notes

Set-Up

OUT: Bride's Parents

Shot

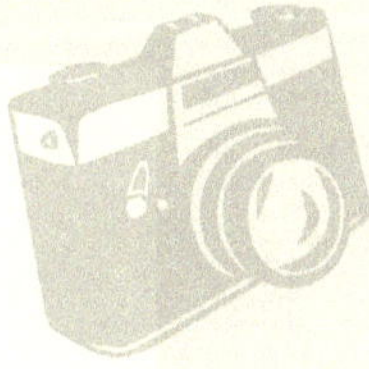

Bride and Groom with his Parents

Notes

Set-Up

IN: Groom's Family

Shot

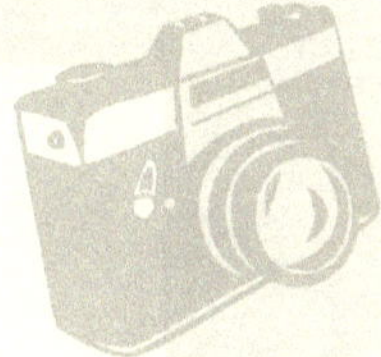

Bride and Groom with his Family

Notes

Set-Up

IN: Bride's Family

Shot

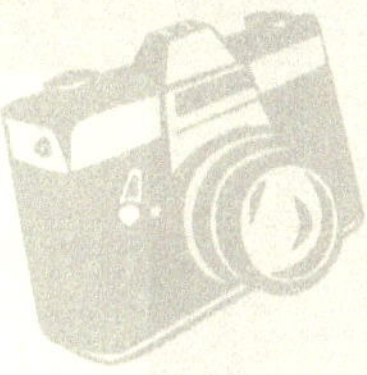

Bride and Groom with both Families

Notes

Set-Up

OUT: Groom's Family

Shot

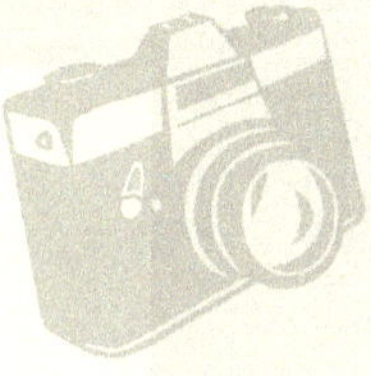

Bride and Groom with her Family

Notes

Set-Up

OUT: Bride's Family
IN: Entire Wedding Party

Shot

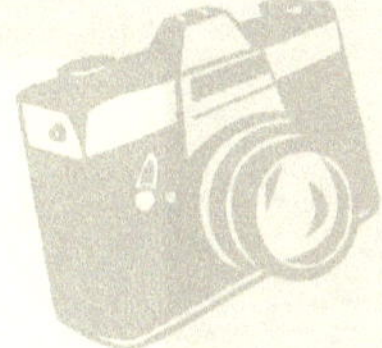

Entire Wedding Party

Notes

Set-Up

OUT: Ladies to the side and wait

Shot

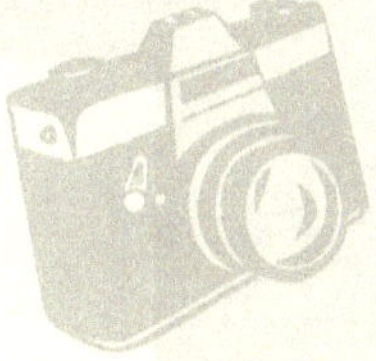

Bride and Groom with men

Notes

Set-Up

OUT: GROOM
To the side and wait

Shot

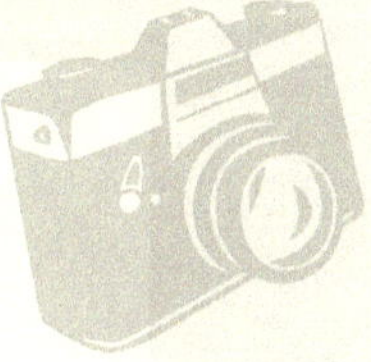

Bride with men

Notes

Set-Up

IN: GROOM
IN: Ladies
OUT: Men

Shot

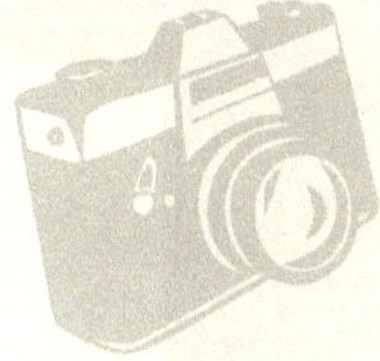

Bride and Groom with Ladies

Notes

OUT: BRIDE
To the side and wait

Shot

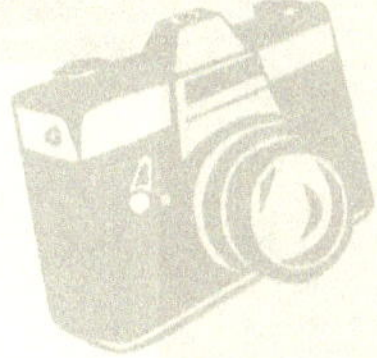

Groom with Ladies

Notes

Set-Up

OUT: Ladies except Maid of Honor
OUT: GROOM
To the side and wait

Shot

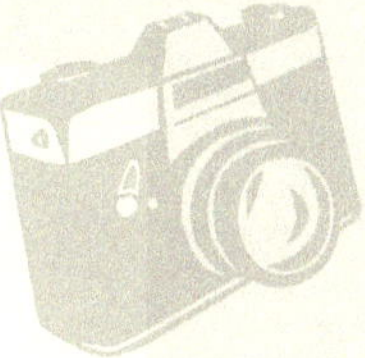

Bride and Maid of Honor

Notes

Set-Up

IN: GROOM

IN: Best Man

Shot

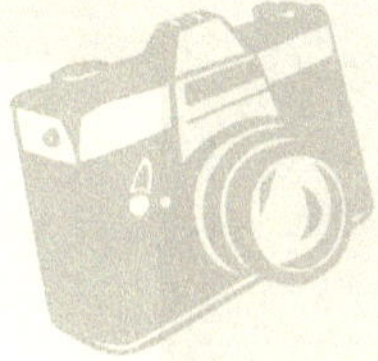

Bride and Groom with Maid
of Honor and Best Man

Notes

Set-Up

OUT: BRIDE
To the side and wait
OUT: Maid of Honor

Shot

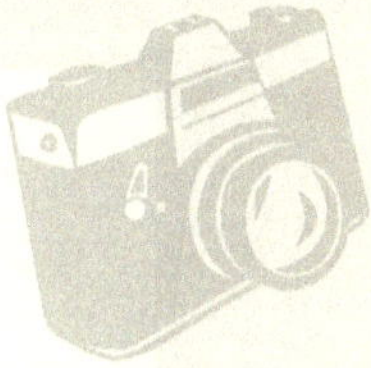

Groom with Best Man

Notes

Set-Up

OUT: Best Man
IN: Groom's Father

Shot

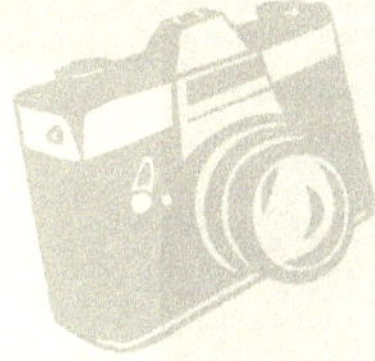

Groom with Dad

Notes

Set-Up

IN: Groom's Mother

Shot

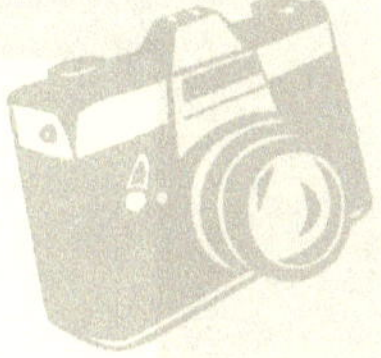

Groom with Mom and Dad

Notes

Set-Up

OUT: Groom's Father

Shot

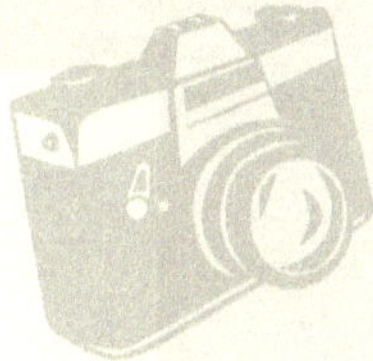

Groom with Mom

Notes

Set-Up

OUT: Groom's Mother
IN: Groom's Brothers and Sisters

Shot

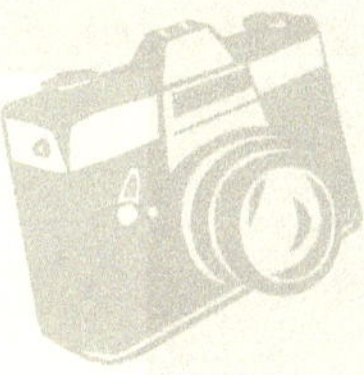

Groom with his Brothers and Sisters

Notes

Set-Up

OUT: All
IN: BRIDE
IN: Bride's Mother

Shot

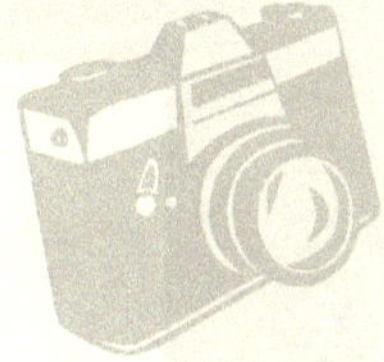

Bride with her Mom

Notes

Set-Up

IN: Bride's Father

Shot

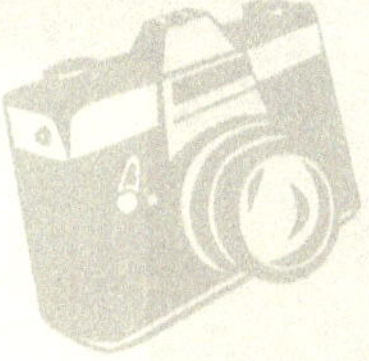

Bride with her Parents

Notes

Set-Up

OUT: Bride's Mother

Shot

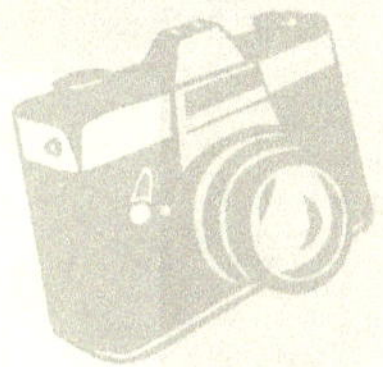

Bride with her Dad

Notes

Set-Up

OUT: Bride's Father
IN: Bride's Brothers and Sisters

Shot

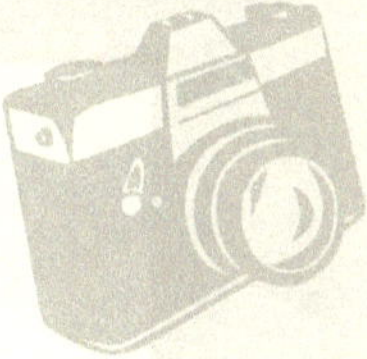

Bride with Brothers and Sisters

Notes

Set-Up

OUT: All except Bride
IN: GROOM
IN: Grandparents

Shot

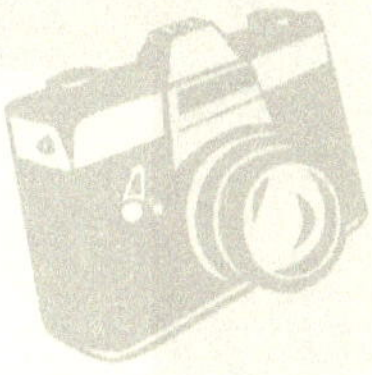

Bride and Groom with Grandparents

Notes

Set-Up

OUT: BRIDE

OUT: GROOM

Shot

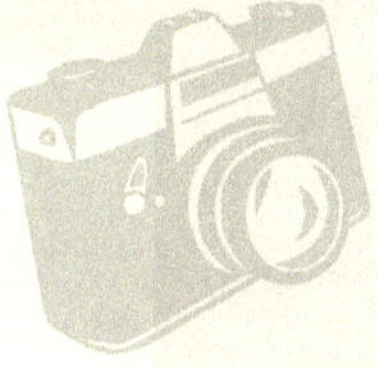

Grandparents

Notes

Set-Up

**OUT: Grandparents;
Move Bride and Groom to window
light or other nearby location**

Shot

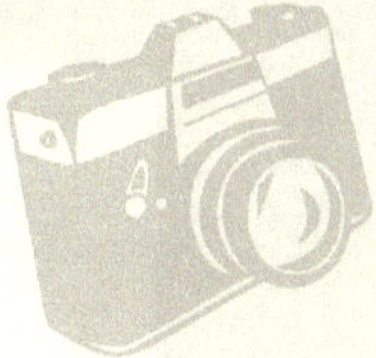

Shots of Bride and Groom
alone or together

Notes

Set-Up

Go to the Reception

Shot

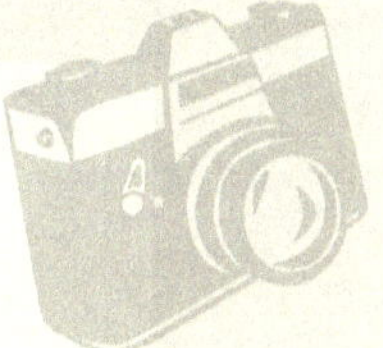

Notes

Set-Up

Shot

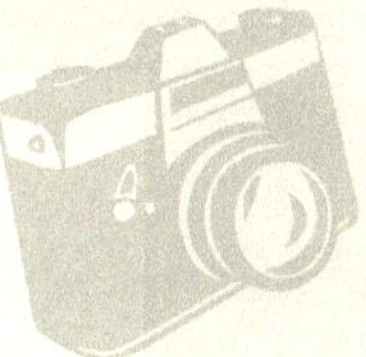

Notes